The Great Barrier Reef

The Great Barrier Reef
A Treasure in the Sea

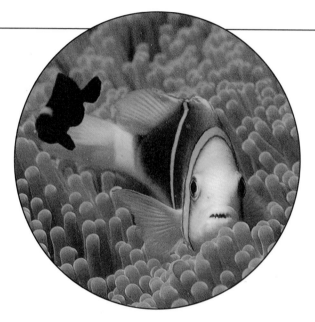

by Alice Gilbreath

HOUGHTON MIFFLIN COMPANY   BOSTON

Atlanta   Dallas   Geneva, Illinois   Palo Alto   Princeton   Toronto

To Sam, Jan, Ron, Debbie, and Karen

Contents

Photographs are reproduced through the courtesy of the A.N.T. Photo Library (Bill Bachman, photographer); the Australian Information Service (J. Fitzpatrick, Neil Murray, Bob Nicol, W. Pederson, photographers); the Australian Tourist Commission (David Beal, photographer); EarthViews (Robert Commer, Ken Howard, Jacki Kilbride, photographers); the Florida News Bureau; the National Archives; the National Oceanic and Atmospheric Administration; Lynn Stone; the U.S. Fish and Wildlife Service (George Harrison, photographer); and WaterHouse (Marty Snyderman, photographer). Cover: underwater corals on the Great Barrier Reef.

# Great Barrier Reef Facts

Location:

Near the northeast coast of Australia

Length:

1,250 miles (2,000 kilometers)

Area:

80,000 square miles (208,000 square kilometers)

Part of Reef Underwater:

90 percent

Temperature of Water:

68°F (20°C) and higher

Built by:

Coral polyps

Kinds of Fish:

More than 1,400 species

First Inhabitants:

Australian Aborigines

First European to Explore and Chart Reef:

Captain James Cook

Number of Visitors Each Year:

Hundreds of thousands

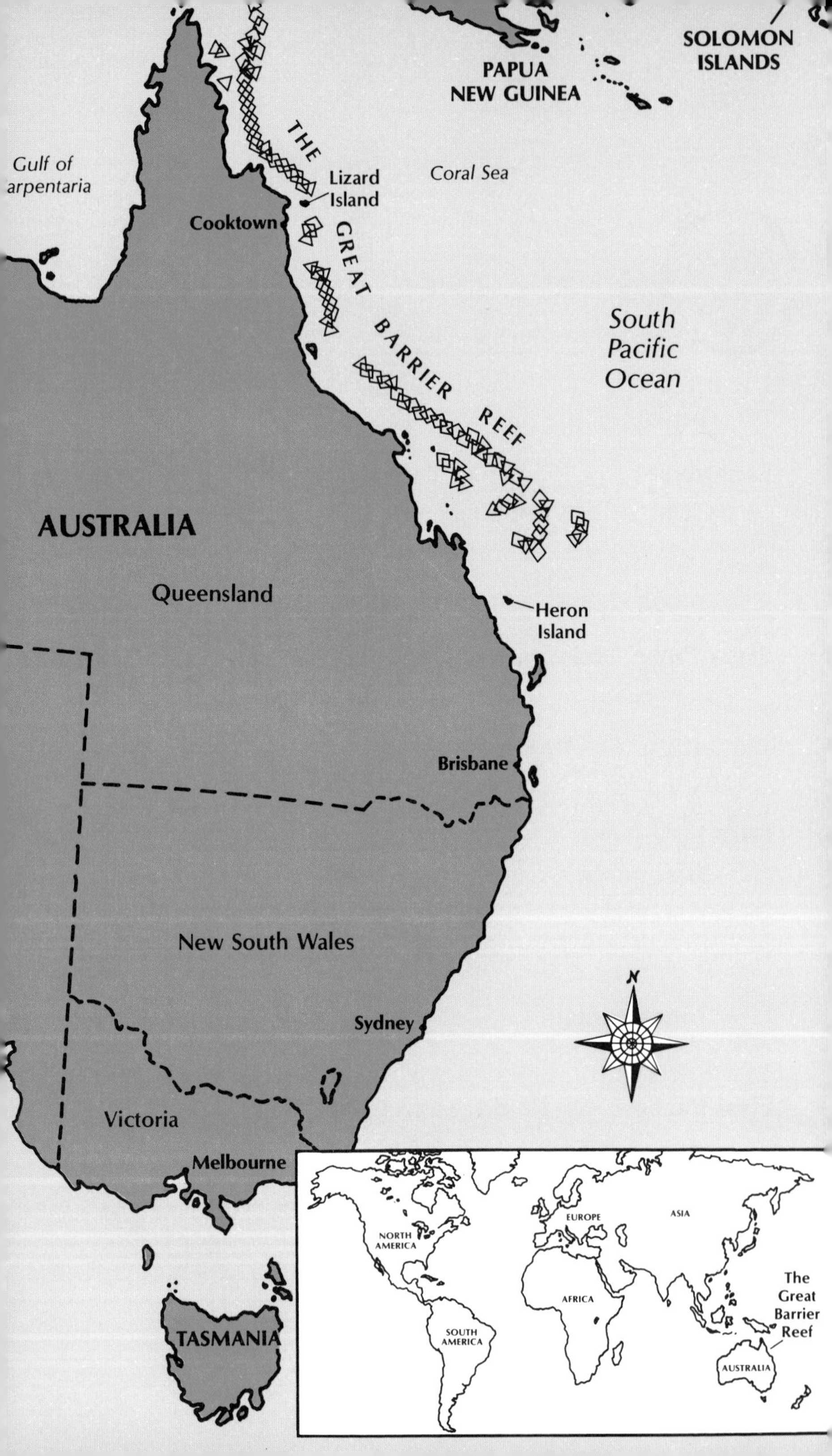

SOLOMON ISLANDS
PAPUA NEW GUINEA
THE GREAT BARRIER REEF
Gulf of arpentaria
Lizard Island
Coral Sea
Cooktown
South Pacific Ocean
AUSTRALIA
Queensland
Heron Island
Brisbane
New South Wales
N
Sydney
Victoria
Melbourne
TASMANIA
NORTH AMERICA
EUROPE
ASIA
AFRICA
SOUTH AMERICA
The Great Barrier Reef
AUSTRALIA

 # The Amazing Corals

Corals have changed the surface of the earth more than any other creature except people. At the Great Barrier Reef, corals have helped create a unique world of marvelous **ecosystems*** where sea and land animals depend on each other.

The Great Barrier Reef lies near the northeast coast of Australia. It was constructed by **billions** of corals—simple creatures ranging from the size of a fingernail to that of a pinhead. Together, these tiny coral animals, known as coral polyps, have built a 1,250-mile-long (2,000-kilometer-long) city in the sea.

The Great Barrier Reef is not a solid wall. It is a long chain of broken reefs with deep channels, **lagoons,** shallow pools, underwater caves, and ledges. Some reefs are very small, no larger than a table top. Others cover a twenty-square-mile (fifty-two-square-kilometer) area. Placed in the United States, they would stretch all the way from New York City to Chicago.

*Words in **bold type** are explained in the glossary at the end of this book.

This enormous living **breakwater** is one of the wonders of the world. It is the largest reef on earth, and may also be the world's most beautiful structure. In some places the reef lies just 10 miles (16 kilometers) from the Australian coast. In other places it lies as far away as 150 miles (241 kilometers). An ocean channel separates the reef from the mainland.

Scientists believe the Great Barrier Reef began to be built long ago during the **Ice Age**. At that time the Pacific Ocean's surface was much lower than it is now because so much water was frozen in the giant ice caps. In the shallow, sunlit waters, corals grew up and out from the Australian **continental shelf**. Then, as ice melted and water ran into the ocean, coral polyps kept reaching toward the light. As each generation of coral animals built upon the last, the reef grew higher and higher. Finally, as more and more ice melted, the ocean rose high enough to separate the long reef chain from the Australian continent.

A Wall Against the Sea

The Great Barrier Reef forms a sturdy wall against the force of the Pacific Ocean. Day after day, it is battered by ocean waves that have built up tremen-

In this aerial view of the Great Barrier Reef, parts of the long reef chain rise up through the clear blue ocean waters.

dous speed. It is a true barrier reef.

The secret of the reef's sturdiness is the way coral, plant life, and ocean waves work together. Waves destroy the weak parts of the reef. Corals and plant life thrive in this **oxygen-rich water** and constantly replace whatever is destroyed. **Algae** binds the living coral to dead coral skeletons and to shell, **sediment**, and other leftover marine materials. These natural processes of destruction, growth, and binding together help form the strong walls of the reef.

The lee side—the side sheltered from the wind— of the Great Barrier Reef faces the Australian mainland. Protected by the reef, waters here are peaceful and quiet. Corals grow abundantly, and many kinds of ocean life find homes in these waters. Within the reef, itself, lie countless openings of different shapes and sizes. These become living quarters for many sea creatures.

Building a Coral Reef

Coral reefs can build only in warm water. The reef ends where the water temperature falls below 68°F (20°C). Hard corals, of which the reef is built, can live only where sunlight can reach them. In order to grow,

A bright yellow fish swims among the abundant underwater corals at the Great Barrier Reef.

coral polyps need sunlight, certain **nutrients**, or kinds of food, and fixed levels of salt and oxygen content in seawater. Corals also need clear water. Too much sediment cuts off light and smothers the tiny creatures.

Reef building coral polyps are small and simple animals hidden inside rocklike skeletons of **lime**. Flowerlike in appearance, they are nothing more than a tube closed at one end and surrounded by tiny

tentacles at the other. Growing on underwater banks, the sides of cliffs, and in shallow valleys and caves, they seem to "bloom" in brilliant colors.

Low-lying coral islands, or **cays**, were formed as corals built up and broke through the ocean's surface. Then, sand and other materials began to collect on the corals. Seeds landed and grew, and plants held the sand in place. Finally the cays became large enough to support forests, birds, and other forms of life.

Coral Polyps

Early in life, as **larvae**, coral polyps drift and tumble in the ocean. They are part of the large pastures of **plankton**—the tiny, mostly **microscopic** animals and plants that float in the ocean. Almost invisible hairs on the bodies of these coral larvae create currents that help move them along. As they drift with the plankton, many become food for other creatures.

Finally, at the age of about ten days, the surviving larvae settle on a smooth surface. They develop tentacles and begin to **secrete** outer skeletons that will fasten them to the reef. Each coral polyp takes **calcium** from the ocean and changes it into lime. Using this rocky substance, it builds a cuplike home.

Once settled, coral polyps remain in the same place for life. They are attached to a permanent structure of dead coral that contains the skeletons of their ancestors. Billions of coral polyps form colorful colonies of many shapes.

Most reef-making corals bud off, or grow out from, the older generation at the top or sides. Each tiny yellow, pink, orange, blue, or green animal becomes part of the reef's rainbow of colors just below the water's surface. Colorful soft corals with flexible skeletons grow in deeper waters, but they are not reef builders.

Each coral polyp has a ring of tentacles equipped with tiny **nettle-cells**. With these stinging cells, it shoots its **prey**— microscopic shrimplike creatures— with poison. Then the coral's tentacles bring this food to its mouth.

Islands, Reefs, and Sea Homes

Not all of the islands in the Great Barrier Reef were formed by corals. Some, like Lizard Island, were once part of the Australian mainland. Lizard Island is a peak of an ancient mountain range. As the mountains were covered by the sea, corals built onto them.

These blue-green coral polyps are attached to a permanent structure of dead coral that contains the skeletons of their ancestors. (Ken Howard/ EarthViews)

Brilliantly colored soft corals such as this one grow in deeper waters but are not reef builders. (Jacki Kilbride/EarthViews)

Many of the Great Barrier Reef's more than 2,000 reefs are not true barriers. Even today, we do not know the exact location of all the reefs. In fact, some of the reefs and islands are still uncharted because they are too dangerous for boats to go through.

Throughout its long chain of reefs and islands, the Great Barrier Reef provides homes for hundreds of sea creatures in lagoons, caves, and **crevices**. Although the reef is a huge and balanced natural system, it can be easily harmed or even destroyed. If we leave it alone, it thrives. If we tamper with it, its delicate ecosystems can break down.

Captain Cook Arrives

Australian Aborigines—the reef's earliest inhabitants—probably lived on the Great Barrier Reef for several thousand years during the Ice Age. Dry land on the reef covered much more area during that cold time in earth history. When the ice melted, seawater gradually flooded the land.

Scientists believe that most of the Aborigines moved to higher ground on the mainland as the rising ocean covered much of their reef home. They probably went back to the reef to hunt for fish, turtles, crabs, and other sea creatures.

But some Aborigines remained on the Great Barrier Reef. Pictures that they and their ancestors drew on the walls of caves and rocks are still there. The Aborigines lived on some of the islands and hunted on some of the others. The barbs in their spears were from stringrays' tails, and their fishing hooks were eagles' claws. They ate nesting birds and their eggs and hunted dugong, a marine mammal. Over two hundred years ago, when the first

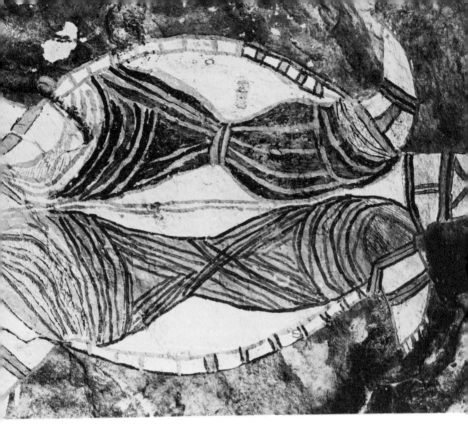

Aborigines hunted turtles on the islands of the Great Barrier Reef. They drew pictures on cave walls such as the one shown above.

European explorers arrived, the Aborigines were there to meet them.

Captain James Cook

The head of the first European expedition to the Great Barrier Reef was Captain James Cook. Cook, a quiet, kindly man, was probably the finest navigator of his time. In 1768 he directed work on *Endeavour*, the flat-bottomed wooden ship, to prepare it for a trip around the world. The ship was 106 feet (32 meters) long and 29 feet (9 meters) wide. Only a few of the rooms on the *Endeavour* were high enough for Captain Cook. At more than 6 feet (nearly 2 meters) in height, the British captain was too tall to stand up straight in most parts of his ship!

Captain Cook was well qualified for this voyage. He had learned to navigate in tugboat-sized North Sea coasters that carried coal to London. Sailing these coasters required more skill than sailing ocean-going vessels. The larger vessels stayed well away from land, while the coasters sailed nearer the shore where tides or winds could drive them onto land. Storms could dash them to pieces. Only skilled sailors could survive such dangers.

With Captain Cook in command, the *Endeavour* sailed from England across the Atlantic Ocean. It traveled down the east coast of South America, rounded Cape Horn, and went on to Tahiti. Then Cook gave orders to head south and west in search of the "Unknown Southern Land." His ship circled New Zealand, and then sailed on to Australia.

In 1770 Captain Cook took the *Endeavour* up the

Captain James Cook was the leader of the first expedition to explore Australia's east coast and the Great Barrier Reef.

east coast of Australia where no European had sailed before. He carefully mapped 2,000 miles (3,200 kilometers) of Australia's coastline and claimed it for his country, Great Britain.

Disaster on the Reef

Sailing along this part of the Australian coast was extremely dangerous. Here, swift currents met, and coral reefs were a neverending danger. Living corals on top of the reefs were never far from the bottom of the ship. Local divers often dived beneath the *Endeavour* to determine the distance between the corals and the ship. In that way Cook hoped to prevent the sharp coral reefs from slicing into the ship's bottom. Sometimes the British sailors moved ahead in small boats and **plumbed** the depths with weighted lines to be sure the ship could pass through safely. Along the Australian coast, this slow **sounding** was done for 1,700 miles (2,735 kilometers).

Suddenly, in spite of all safety measures, the ship met with disaster. With a grind and a roar, the *Endeavour* struck a coral reef. The ship's bow rose, and then dropped hard. Lines snapped. When one of the main masts snapped off, sailors fell to the decks. The coral reef ripped through the ship and grounded it.

Captain Cook rushed to help the sailor at the wheel. He knew that no one was near enough to help the *Endeavour* and its crew. They would not be missed for many months, and even then, no one would know where to look for them. To reach the mainland, twenty miles (thirty-two kilometers) away, they would have to save their ship.

The man standing on the bow of this boat is "plumbing" the depth of the water in much the same way as Captain Cook's crew "sounded" passages throughout the Great Barrier Reef.

Captain Cook ordered the crew to pump water over the side as fast as possible and lighten the ship by throwing heavy items overboard. After the anchors were dropped, sailors dumped six swivel guns and all the firewood and empty casks into the ocean. They carried iron and stone **ballast** up from the hold and pushed it over the rail. All day long they worked. Pumping was so exhausting that each man could work no more than ten minutes without collapsing on the deck. Finally, that night, the *Endeavour* floated free.

But now the ship was taking on water faster than the pumps could move it out. At Captain Cook's command, the crew laid a sail on deck and poured on **pitch**, oil, and **oakum** to help waterproof it. Then they lowered the sail over the side and moved it into place under the ship's hull. They tied it in place like a big bandage. Inrushing water helped to hold the sail against the hole.

With the sail in place, one pump could keep up with the incoming waters. Then, when the tide came again, the ship made it to the beach. Captain Cook and his crew were grateful to be alive and to have a ship that could be repaired.

"Cook's Passage"

Six weeks later, after the *Endeavour* was again sailable, Captain Cook climbed to the top of a mountain on Lizard Island. From the mountain he hoped to see the ocean beyond the reefs and find a passageway to get his battered ship out of the dangerous corals. Cook looked at the dark water where there were channels. He looked, also, at the lighter colored water where the coral reefs rose nearly to the ocean's surface. A few miles away was a sight that would discourage most sailors. Captain Cook called it a "line of dreadful surf." Here, huge waves suddenly came to a halt as they battered the outer reef barrier.

Cook continued to study the area along the outer reef barrier. Finally, he located some narrow breaks in this coral wall. It was through these breaks that he managed to sail the ship safely out to sea. This route is now called "Cook's passage."

Before Captain Cook sailed the *Endeavour* back to England, he claimed the southern continent for his country. By mapping the Australian coastline, he left a guide for future captains who attempted to sail their ships through these dangerous waters.

Not all ships exploring the rugged Great Barrier Reef have been as fortunate as Captain Cook and the crew of the *Endeavour*. More than 500 vessels have shipwrecked on the reef.

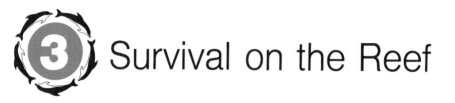

3 Survival on the Reef

An angelfish twists and turns, flashing its colors. It is sending a message to nearby sea creatures: "This is my territory and I'll fight to defend it." Seeing the angelfish, an approaching fish swims away.

Living space is a problem for most reef animals. Like the angelfish, many are **territorial** and will not allow other creatures to come near. These "homeowners" must remain alert at all times to keep out invaders.

Young ocean creatures have a difficult time finding homes. Some take over living space by fighting for it. Others move in immediately when another creature dies. As coral animals add new parts to the Great Barrier Reef, homeless creatures move into cracks and crevices. All the time sea animals are looking for living quarters, they must find food and avoid **predators**.

Camouflaged Creatures

Some animals survive because they blend in with their surroundings. Brilliant colors can **camouflage**

An angelfish flashes its bright colors to signal to other creatures that this is its own special living space. (Robert Commer/EarthViews)

fish among the brightly colored corals. Sometimes, a fish's outline is broken up by bands, patches, and spots. This is another means of camouflage. Some creatures even change color to match their surroundings.

Since in the lagoons there is no place to hide, camouflage is even more important. Here, an animal benefits from having dull colors. Brightly colored fish could be seen easily by predators and would not survive for long. Like the brightly colored camouflage of reef creatures, the lagoon animals' camouflage is not always used for protection. It is also used to aid in hunting for food. Animals living on and in the reef compete with each other for food. They use many disguises and tricks that help them capture their prey.

Camouflage aids the octopus in its search for food. This cave-dwelling animal can change color almost instantly from brown to white to green to red. Its bag-shaped body is surrounded by eight long arms, or tentacles, that hang in a circle from its head.

The wobbegong, or carpet shark, is disguised by gray and brown colors. Tentacles around its upper lip look like seaweeds. In the lagoons its drab colors and its "seaweed" look present a perfect camouflage. The

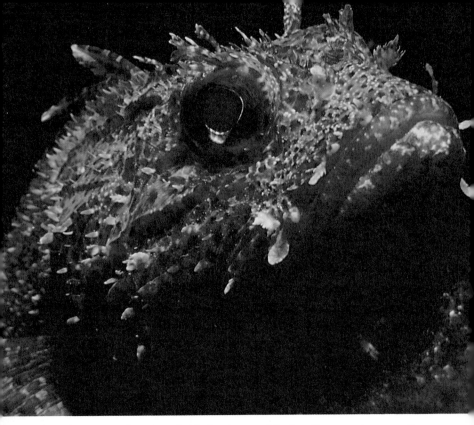

The features of a stonefish's body provide it with expert camouflage. This remarkable fish even bends its body to conform to the shape of the rock it rests against. (Robert Commer/EarthViews)

wobbegong waits for its prey to swim by, and then lunges out to grab a meal.

The ten-inch-long (twenty-six-centimeter-long) stonefish is camouflaged with warts and green algae along its stone-shaped body. When a tiny fish swims nearby, the stonefish suddenly opens its large mouth. That quick movement creates a current that brings in its food.

Attached to the underside of a large shark, a remora hitchhikes through the waters of the Great Barrier Reef.

Finding Food

The ribbon-shaped remora, or sucker fish, survives in a different way. With its suction cup mouth, it fastens itself to the manta ray or another large fish and rides along with the big fish. Its suction pads have backward-sloping slats. When the big fish moves through the water, pressure fastens the remora even more firmly to its host. When the host fish eats, the remora drops off long enough to feed on the scraps. Though the remora is a good swimmer, its best method of getting food is to hitch a ride on a larger fish.

The trumpetfish has an unusual way of finding food. It feeds on small fish and shrimp that are passed by by larger fish. Since the small creatures are not eaten by the larger fish, they remain quiet when they pass. The trumpetfish hides itself by swimming directly above a larger fish. Then, swiftly, it swoops down on a shrimp or small fish and has a meal.

Some reef creatures use poison to obtain food. Tentacles of the bell-shaped sea wasp, or box jellyfish, have stinging cells. During the summer months, these creatures are brought to the reef from the open ocean by northerly winds. The sea wasp uses its stinging cells to **paralyze** shrimplike prawns and other small creatures. Lionfish use their feathery fins to inject poison that kills the small creatures they feed on. They use the same poison to defend themselves.

Protection from Predators

Like the lionfish, most creatures need protection from predators. On the Great Barrier Reef, many have unusual ways of protecting themselves.

An inch-long (two-and-a-half-centimeter-long) sea slug, the nudibranch, is well protected even though it has no shell. By eating the poisonous cells of sea anemones, it acquires a poison of its own. The poison does not affect the nudibranch's slimy **digestive system**. As this beautiful sea slug moves along the corals, its body coloring says "stay away" to would-be predators. If necessary, the nudibranch stings a predator with its brightly colored tentacles.

Sea urchins use long **spines** for protection. In addition to pricking or poisoning a predator, these spines can lock an urchin tightly in a coral crevice. Small fish sometimes hide from predators among a sea urchin's spines.

The female gall crab is about the size of the tip of a person's little finger. This tiny crab chooses a coral and stays on it until the coral builds around her, walling her in permanently. Here she can lay her eggs in safety. Currents bring in her supply of food. The male crab, much smaller than the female, lives in a separate coral but is small enough to come and go.

Some creatures, such as starfish, survive by re-growing arms that predators snatch. The brittle star

If threatened by another sea creature, the nudibranch stings the preda-tor with its brightly colored tentacles. (Marty Snyderman/WaterHouse)

simply casts off whichever arm a predator grabs and then grows another to take its place. Crabs, too, can grow new limbs. They often escape from predators when one of their limbs breaks off.

The Reef's Sea Teams

Two animals sometimes become a team in order to help both creatures. They join together in a relationship called **symbiosis**. One of the most interesting sea teams is made up of a "cleaning station" and a "customer" that comes to be cleaned.

The four-inch-long (ten-centimeter-long) wrasse is exactly the size that larger fish like to eat. But the wrasse is safe around the big fish. It does a kind of dance that shows off its black stripes and blue color. This dance tells its customers that the little fish has set up a cleaning station.

Larger fish, bothered constantly by **parasites**, come to be cleaned. The little wrasse eats the parasites from their entire bodies, even inside their mouths and on the outer part of wounds. When the cleaning job is finished, the big fish feel better, and the wrasse has had a meal. Cleaning stations never lack customers. The bigger fish show that they want the little fish's cleaning service by hovering with mouths open, fins fanned, and gill-covers puffed.

One fish, the blenny, takes advantage of the cleaning stations. It has colors much like those of the wrasse. Sometimes a blenny fools a bigger fish into thinking it is a cleaner fish. Then it snatches a piece of the big fish's **gill** or fin and dashes for cover.

The banded coral shrimp, a small **crustacean**, has a different kind of cleaning service. It perches on a coral and signals with its **antennae** that it is ready for business. Then, with its fuzzy pincers, or claws, it picks parasites off of each of its finned customers.

The sea anemone and the clownfish help each other to survive. The sea anemone is a beautiful but deadly trap. Its stinging tentacles kill fish and also protect the creature from enemies such as sea slugs. The orange and black clownfish, however, is not harmed by the sea anemone. This fish's body is covered with a slime that seems to protect it as it darts in and out among the anemone's tentacles. If another fish swims in to grab the clownfish, the anemone kills the invader. Then the clownfish feeds on scraps of the anemone's food. Sometimes the clownfish darts out to grab a shrimp or tiny fish, then dashes back to the

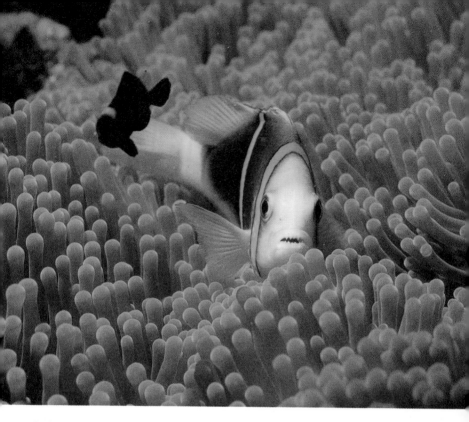

Safe in its sea home, a clownfish darts in and out among the stinging tentacles of the anemone. (Robert Commer/EarthViews)

safety of the anemone's tentacles to eat it. At these times the anemone probably feeds on the scraps of the clownfish's meal.

A snapping shrimp and a goby fish often become a team, too. The shrimp does not see well, but is an excellent digger. The goby cannot dig but needs a burrow. Working together, the shrimp digs a burrow while the goby props itself up on its fins and stands guard at the burrow's entrance. If danger approaches, a flick of the goby's tail warns the shrimp, and both creatures dive into the burrow.

Among the cracks, crevices, caves, and lagoons of the Great Barrier Reef, sea animals have developed special ways to find food and protection from predators. For reef creatures these skills are needed each day in order to survive.

# The Daytime Reef

Loud shrieking, twittering, groaning, and screeching begin on the Great Barrier Reef at dawn during the summer months. These are the voices of shearwaters, or mutton birds, the reef's alarm clocks. Soon their cries are joined by those of other seabirds. Until the birds leave to find food, their songs make the reef a very noisy place.

At dawn, too, the dreaded moray eel, a night hunter, swims into a coral cave to rest. Even during daylight hours, it may grab a passing fish. Other night creatures, too, now find places to sleep in caves, crevices, and tiny holes. Most corals close their tentacles and stay in hiding during the daytime hours.

As the temperature rises on the reef, plant plankton, or **phytoplankton**, change the sun's energy into food for ocean creatures. Phytoplankton are the beginning of the ocean's food chain. These microscopic plants are eaten by tiny animals, called **zooplankton**, that become part of the plankton "meadows" in the

Resting in its coral cave home, a moray eel remains ready to grab a passing fish for a quick meal. (Robert Commer/EarthViews)

sea. Eggs of many animals float in and become part of the plankton for a short time. Hatching larvae of various creatures do, too. The plankton meadows furnish food for many animals, including some **species** of whales.

The daytime reef teems with life both below and above water. More than 1,400 species of fish, alone, live on the Great Barrier Reef. Every tiny area of land

The daytime reef teems with life. Every tiny crack and crevice is the home of some reef creature.

or water in and on the reef is the home of some creature, and often more than one. These animals spend
their lives laying eggs, defending their territories,
and playing the game of hide and seek—seeking to
find food without becoming food for predators.

Islands and Beaches

The centers of many Great Barrier Reef islands
are covered with dense plant growth. Groves of
prickly pandanus trees scatter their leaves and
orange-colored fruit over the islands. Air-rooted or-
chids cling to the pandanus trees.

Pisonias, trees that grow fifty feet (fifteen meters) high, provide shade from the scorching sun.
They also provide perching spots for the white heron
and other birds. But the pisonias' sticky seed buds
can be dangerous to nesting birds. Sometimes these
seed buds glue a bird's feathers together so tightly
that it can no longer fly.

At the beach, white sand glistens. Below the
sand's surface, ghost crabs stay safely hidden in their
burrows. Dog whelks—snails in spiral shells—eat the
remains of other creatures' meals left on the sand.
Their keen sense of smell leads them to their food.

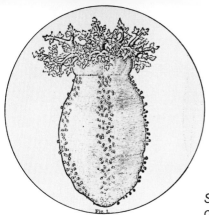

Sea cucumbers remove little pieces of food from grains of sand.

Often, dog whelks move about just below the surface of the sand.

These large marine snails lay eggs protected by tough cases that form strings of coin-shaped disks. After the eggs hatch, the whelk larvae stay in the plankton meadows for long periods. Many of the larvae become food for other creatures.

Life on the Reef Flats

At low tide, patches of the reef's coral, known as the reef flats, or platform, rise above the water for a short time. Because the water near the reef is now shallow, reef creatures are easier to see. **Shoals**, or groups, of tiny fish dart here and there as one body. On the reef platform, sea cucumbers, slimy, sausage-shaped animals, eat grains of sand. As the sand passes through their bodies, the sea cucumbers remove little pieces of food from it.

On the reef platform, a clam holds its shell open. This allows water to pass through its gills, which filter out bits of food.

As the sun beats down on the reef, sea urchins rest deep in coral crevices. A feather star extends its graceful arms, which have tiny tube feet, to catch food brought to it by the water current. Food sticks to its tube feet. Then the food moves up the creature's arms and into its mouth at the base of its body. When a feather star wishes to move on to another area, it allows the current to carry it.

On the outer reef flats, creeping snails and chitons scrape algae from the corals. To gather these razor-thin plants they use tiny teeth in their **radula**, or ribbonlike tongues. As the tide moves in, more and more of the reef flats are covered with water. Soon the ocean again washes over the reef platform.

Underwater Beauty

The greatest beauty of the Great Barrier Reef lies underwater. Hundreds of kinds of coral form huge, colorful forests. The coral forests provide homes for fish—red, blue, gold, and black—that are just as colorful as the corals.

Batfish and coral trout flash their colors, which blend with their surroundings. Clownfish hover among the tentacles of the beautiful but deadly sea anemone.

An angelfish circles a rock and watches the borders of its territory. A scorpion fish, camouflaged in

A colorful, close-up scene of some of the forms of life found on the Great Barrier Reef.

coral, waits for small fish and other ocean creatures to come along. Then it opens its lower jaw and sucks them in. Divers have learned to stay away from the scorpion fish. If stepped on, poison from its spines can cause much pain.

At greater depths, where sunlight does not reach, hard corals cannot live. Soft ones, such as fan corals, thrive here and show their rainbows of glowing colors. Far below the surface of the sea, there are fewer fish than in the shallow waters around the reef. A large manta ray swims and banks swiftly, moving almost like a flying bird.

A damselfish lays her sticky eggs on a branch of fan coral. The male will guard the eggs until they hatch. When damselfish are chased by a predator, the smaller fish finds safety among these coral branches.

Lagoon Life

In the lagoon, fish have no place to hide. Here the fish do not have the bright colors of those that live among the corals. Instead, most are gray or black on top so that they blend with the water when viewed from above. Underneath, they are whitish to blend with the water's surface when seen from below.

The fish in the reef lagoons band together in shoals for safety. Because there are so many fish in a shoal, they appear as a "blizzard" of fish. When they locate food, such as a shoal of smaller fish, the larger fish swim rapidly through it. As they pass through, they eat many of the smaller creatures. In turn, their numbers decrease when a shoal of even larger fish passes through their shoal.

Mackerel, herring, and mullet feed on shoals of smaller fish, while black-tip sharks and barracuda hunt mackerel, herring, and mullet. Snappers patrol the lagoon channel looking for likely prey.

On the Great Barrier Reef, daytime brings forth a nonstop, colorful parade of life. Before the day is over, many creatures will have found meals at the expense of other creatures. Eggs will be laid. Others will hatch. All the action is part of the rhythm of life on the great reef.

The Reef at Night

At dusk many changes take place quietly on the reef. Day creatures hunt for safe places to spend the night. Night creatures come out of caves and crevices to look for food. For the reef animals it is like a changing of shifts. The "night shift" takes over the same areas in the reef that the "day shift" has just left. Often, day creatures go into the same hiding places that night creatures left minutes before.

When darkness falls on the cays and islands, seabirds return from their food-hunting trips. Reef herons go to roost. Shearwaters go into their burrows or spend the night squatting outside them. At the beach silver gulls hover in the air, looking for another meal.

Searching for Food

The sand seems to come alive at night. The ghost crab comes out of its burrow and searches on the beach for food. The crab's eyes are built in a special way that allows it to see in all directions at the same

A ghost crab uses its periscopelike eyes to check for bits and pieces of food left by day creatures. (George Harrison)

time. With these periscopelike eyes, it checks for bits and pieces of food left by day creatures. Sometimes it picks the bones left by animals that are the crab's enemies. While the ghost crab usually eats scraps, it will also grab a newly hatched sea turtle. When danger threatens, the ghost crab runs rapidly across the sand and scoots into its burrow. At dawn, it retires to its burrow for the day, leaving nothing but a fresh mound of sand to mark its tunnel entrance.

In the darkness soft-bodied hermit crabs come out of the undergrowth at the beach's edge. Moving about in borrowed shells, their pincers search the tide for bits of food. Since they spend their entire lives in another creature's shell, they must move each time they outgrow their present "home." Moving from one home to another is very dangerous for the hermit crab. Usually, it moves its present shell next to its new shell home. Then it transfers quickly from the old shell to the new.

At night it is safer for corals to feed. Most of their predators are day creatures that are not active after dark. Since corals cannot move from one place to another, they must wait for food to come to them. They filter out the plankton, which thrive in the warm, sunlit waters around coral reefs. As corals reach out their tentacles to feed, the reef "blossoms" into huge flower gardens.

After dark many tiny animals—the zooplankton—come out of their daytime hiding places. They rise into shallow water to feed on the phytoplankton. While they feed, they become part of the plankton. Many will be eaten by night creatures. At dawn those that have survived the night will again go into hiding. Because some zooplankton glow in the dark, their movement in the water causes starlike sparkles of light.

Most fish, like many other reef creatures, are not active at night. These fish swim into coral crevices for protection while they sleep.

Beautifully colored tube worms look like tiny flowers as they unfold their feeding fans at night. Nudibranches come from under ledges that may be thirty to fifty feet (about nine to fifteen meters) deep. These beautiful creatures come in many shades of yellow, pink, blue, or rose. Some have stripes, spots, or patches. Often, they take on the color of their food as camouflage. Nudibranches feed slowly as they crawl over sponges or algae. They move through the water by rippling the edges of their bodies.

At night on the top part of the reef, marine **mollusks** called cowries come out of crevices in which they have spent the day. The cowries crawl across rough surfaces of coral boulders searching for plant food. They will lay their eggs under these same boulders. Cowries have remarkably polished shells because they have living tissue, called the **mantle**, that can extend up the shells' sides to clean, rub, and polish.

The cowrie has a beautifully polished shell.

Predators and Prey

Night sleepers of the Great Barrier Reef try to protect themselves while they rest. Some parrotfish, which are day creatures, secrete a sticky substance— a kind of sleeping bag—in which to spend the night. This covering gives some protection from moray eels and other predators that use their sense of smell to locate prey.

The octopus comes out of its cave at night to hunt crabs and fish among the corals.

The moray eel is a night prowler. It comes out of its cave at dusk and hunts both night feeders and night sleepers of the reef. The moray eel can pull out reef creatures that are wedged deeply into cracks and crevices. This fearsome-looking animal has knifelike teeth and a viselike grip.

The octopus comes out at night from its daytime cave. From its cave, even as it rests, it grabs passing prey. At night it stalks crabs and fish among the corals.

Big-eyed night creatures, such as the squirrelfish, spend their days in coral caves. At night they come out to feed. Red cardinals, too, leave their caves to feed along the edge of the reef. Angel, butterfly, and surgeon fish—all day creatures—will settle for the night in the same caves left by the squirrelfish and cardinals. For protection, some of these fish may tone down their bright colors while they sleep. The lionfish also hunts at night. It drives its prey into a corner by fanning its threatening fins.

At one time, feather stars probably fed during the day. Perhaps they feed at night now because their predators are not so numerous. At dusk these flower-like animals come out from under clumps of coral. They open to feed from the surrounding seawater.

The spiny sea urchin crawls out of the crevice where it spent the day. Moving across the reef on long tube feet, it feeds on algae.

Another night-feeding creature is the five-inch-long (thirteen-centimeter-long) pearl fish. During the day it lives inside a sea cucumber's digestive tube. Here it is safe because it is too large to become food for

The lionfish drives its prey into a corner by fanning its threatening fins. (Robert Commer/EarthViews)

the sea cucumber. At night it goes out to search for food. At the break of day the little pearl fish returns to the safety of the sea cucumber's food tube.

In spite of all the activity—day and night—on the Great Barrier Reef, most animals live their entire lives in a very small area. Only an emergency such as sudden changes in their environment can cause them to leave.

Land Creatures of the Reef

A female green sea turtle climbs from the water onto the sandy beach of Heron Island. Like thousands of other green turtles, she has come here at high tide to lay her eggs. Only the moon lights her way as she drags her 300-pound (136-kilogram) body across the sand.

Turtle Nesting Time

In the ocean, supported by the water, the huge sea turtle moved with ease. On land she moves along slowly and awkwardly with a kind of rowing action. Finally, she reaches the outer edge of heavy vegetation. With great effort, she keeps dragging her heavy body. From time to time she stops and lifts her head in order to breathe.

The sea turtle chooses the best possible place for the nest. She stops at a spot beyond where the highest tide can reach, yet where the sand is moist.

Now her digging begins. With her front flippers working together, she scoops sand and flings it back-

A female green sea turtle searches for a good place to dig her nest on the beach of Heron Island.

ward into piles. Her rear flippers push these piles farther back on the beach. An hour or so later, the nest is crater-shaped and as deep as the turtle is high. Then her rear flippers dig a foot-deep (thirty-one-centimeter-deep) hole near the center of the nest. In it she lays a hundred or more soft, white, rubbery eggs the size of ping-pong balls.

Next the turtle covers the eggs with sand and

Her egg-laying done, a 300-pound (136-kilogram) sea turtle makes her way slowly back to the ocean. (David Beal)

drags her tired body back across the beach. When she reaches the ocean, the water again supports her great weight. Now, for a time, her task is finished. But she will make this same nest-building trip five or six more times during the next few months. In one nesting season she may lay as many as 1,000 eggs.

After the season three or four years will pass before the green sea turtle will return again to land to lay eggs. At that time she probably will come back to the Great Barrier Reef—one of the most important turtle-nesting areas of the world. Since she may live for decades, she will make this trip many times.

Heated by the sun, the beach sand keeps the turtle eggs warm for two to three months. When the eggs hatch, the baby turtles scramble out of their sandy nest as a team.

A Race for Life

Newly hatched turtles are two to three inches (five to eight centimeters) long, blackish on top and white underneath. Once on the beach, they move naturally toward the light reflected by the sea. Artificial lights, though, can cause the baby turtles to become confused. Because they come out of the nest at night, when hotel lights are on, they may find the resort hotel instead of the ocean. On Heron Island, visitors often pick up baby turtles that have lost their bearings and carry them to their sea home.

As they move across the sand, many baby turtles become food for other animals. Gulls can spot them by moonlight. In the darkness ghost crabs become their enemies, too. Though the little turtles are safer after

A baby sea turtle struggles to reach the safety of the sea. (Lynn Stone)

they reach the water, they still can become a meal for a large fish. Of the many turtles newly hatched, only a few will live for the eight years necessary to become adults.

We do not know exactly where these young turtles spend the next few years before returning to the reef's nesting grounds. In coming to the Great Barrier Reef, they travel south from good feeding grounds farther north. These northern feeding grounds are more to their liking but are not good for hatching eggs. How turtles know where to find good nesting grounds remains a mystery.

Not long ago, green turtles of the Great Barrier Reef ended up in a turtle cannery so often that their numbers were few. Now they are protected here.

Turtles form just one part of the millions of creatures that **migrate** to the Great Barrier Reef during the summer season. "Down under" in Australia, summer lasts from December through March. While most of the Great Barrier Reef is underwater at least part of the time, a few square miles remain dry. Like the turtles, seabirds use these dry areas as nesting grounds. Nests are built on even the tiniest cays.

So many birds nest on the cays and islands of the

reef that even the air above them is crowded with birds. Only a small part of the reef can be used for ground nesting because nests must be out of the reach of tides.

Burrowing Birds

The wedge-tailed shearwater, or mutton bird, is dark and pigeon-sized. It solves its nesting problem by going underground. This bird migrates to the Great Barrier Reef from Siberia thousands of miles to the north. Each year in October, millions of wedge-tailed shearwaters arrive at the reef's cays and islands.

Heron Island is a popular nesting ground for these birds. In this sandy soil they dig burrows, some several yards long, near the roots of pisonia trees. Shearwaters hide the small burrow entrances with twigs and leaves. The female lays one egg near the end of the burrow. On treeless cays, these burrows provide shelter. Even when there are many trees and not much space for underground living, shearwaters build their nests underground. During the nesting season, parts of the island are honeycombed with burrows.

After their single egg is laid, shearwater parents take turns keeping the egg warm and going to the

Heron Island is a popular nesting ground for seabirds such as the wedge-tailed shearwater. (W. Pederson)

ocean for food. Later, when their chick is hatched, both parents bring it food.

These seabirds have long, narrow wings that angle forward. Their long bills, curved near the tips, are adapted to catch and eat squid and other small creatures. Adult birds spend their entire day at sea looking for food.

After their young are raised, the shearwater parents fly back to Siberia. A couple of months later, the young birds take off on their own trip to the far north.

While the shearwaters build underground nests, several kinds of terns make small, saucer-shaped holes in the ground in which to lay their eggs. Since many terns nest here, the nests are almost side by side.

Nesting Noddies

Aboveground, in the trees of Heron Island, white-capped noddy terns are also nesting. Using grass and dead leaves, they build somewhat sloppy nests in the pisonia trees. Most nests contain only one egg. When the chick hatches, the tern parents will feed it squid and fish which they catch in the sea.

Nesting noddies are not the least bit quiet. Their harsh screams announce to the world that they are there. These small ocean birds have slender bodies with narrow wings, pointed bills, and forked tails. They are truly at home over the water as they skim the ocean surface for small fish, and then dive to catch them.

As a tern parent comes back from the ocean with food for its chick, it sometimes meets a frigate bird circling high above the nests. This bird is a pirate. It

These terns nest at Michaelmas Cay, a small coral island in the Great Barrier Reef. (J. Fitzpatrick)

flies at the tern, forcing it to spit out its swallowed fish. Then the frigate bird grabs the food in midair.

Frigate birds, too, nest at the Great Barrier Reef. While they are excellent fliers, they can take off only into the wind. As a result, frigate birds must build their nests in places where the wind blows in a certain direction.

In spite of the crowded conditions, the Great Barrier Reef is an excellent place for seabirds to lay eggs and raise their young. Here, on the cays and islands, no large animals disturb them. For a season the seabirds and the green sea turtles add to the abundant life on the reef.

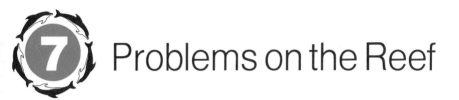

Problems on the Reef

"Starfish are everywhere," said a diver. "They are so thick that I can't count them." He was talking about the crown-of-thorns starfish. This small sea animal has caused a problem on the Great Barrier Reef that overshadows all other problems.

A Population Explosion

In the early 1960s the crown-of-thorns starfish went through a "population explosion." It happened not only at the Great Barrier Reef but in several other places as well. No one can be sure why the numbers of this dinner-plate-sized starfish increased so rapidly.

Some scientists think that the sudden change is part of a **cycle** and will pass. Others believe that too many of the starfish's greatest enemy, the beautiful giant triton shellfish, were removed from the reef by shell collectors. They say that over a ten-year period, as many as 100,000 tritons were taken from the reef. The triton, a large, snaillike animal, can eat its way

The shell of a giant triton shellfish. Many tritons have been removed from the reef by shell collectors. (Bob Nicol)

through the poisonous spines of the crown-of-thorns starfish. A triton eats about one of these starfish per week.

Some scientists point out that blasting and digging out channels in the reef may have made the problem worse. Such activities may have changed the underwater **environment** to one in which the crown-of-thorns starfish can thrive.

Starfish Armies

Like other starfish, the crown-of-thorns was once a night creature that spent its days hidden in a crevice. Since the numbers of these starfish have increased so greatly, the creatures now eat reef corals both day and night. They gather in groups, and then move out in a "feeding frenzy." As they eat, these sixteen-armed starfish armies turn their **gastric sacs**, or stomachs, inside out and cover the corals like a parachute. The starfish's digestive juices **dissolve** the coral, and the creature absorbs its meal, leaving only white coral skeletons. In twelve hours this starfish can destroy forty or fifty years of coral growth.

The hungry crown-of-thorns starfish armies are sometimes 30 feet (9 meters) wide and 300 feet (91 meters) long. Using their sucker-tipped tube feet, they move in an organized group, feeding on corals as they go. A hundred starfish may gather on a patch of coral the size of a small room. They fasten themselves to the coral branches and each other until they look like one giant cactus. Most sea creatures leave these starfish alone because their upper surfaces are covered with dozens of sharp spines that can give off poison.

Today the starfish population explosion con-

A crown-of-thorns starfish attacks coral on the Great Barrier Reef.

tinues. During one month each year, each female crown-of-thorns starfish releases millions of eggs into the water. Here they are **fertilized** and become larvae.

Starfish Predators

Normally, coral polyps eat millions of these larvae. Now, because so many corals have been killed, more starfish larvae survive to become adults. The dead corals even provide more cracks and crevices for the larvae to settle and grow. All these changes on the reef add to the starfish problem.

Another creature, the giant clam, eats many larvae and eggs of the crown-of-thorns starfish. This 500-pound (227-kilogram) clam is believed to live as long as one hundred years. Just one giant clam could, in its lifetime, eat large amounts of these larvae and eggs. But giant clams, too, have been hunted by people. Because of their size and beauty, they have been used as bathroom sinks and for many kinds of decoration. Clam poaching, or illegal hunting, has been a problem for many years. Since the giant clam is becoming an **endangered species**, it no longer helps control the great numbers of crown-of-thorns starfish larvae.

The grouper is another enemy of the crown-of-thorns starfish. This big fish has been difficult for anglers to catch. But since the 1950s, when high-powered outboard motors became popular on the Great Barrier Reef, scuba divers have killed many groupers with spearguns. Like the giant clam and the triton, the grouper faces a threat from humans.

Living staghorn coral grows at this place on the Great Barrier Reef. All parts of a reef may be destroyed after crown-of-thorns starfish feed on the hard corals. (Neil Murray)

Repairing the Damage

The crown-of-thorns starfish has invaded several parts of the Great Barrier Reef. In some places armies of starfish have killed most of the hard corals on an entire reef. Then they move on to feed on other reefs.

Where large areas of corals are killed, the **ecology** of the reef changes. Within two or three weeks, algae covers the dead, white coral. Then the nearby coral larvae have no places left to settle and grow. Reefs may break down because no new growth occurs. Ocean waves **erode** the weakening reef barriers. **Cyclones** tear at the reef almost every year and add to the damage. And in some places, after hard coral begins to grow on a damaged reef, the crown-of-thorns starfish again moves in and destroys it.

The starfish problem is truly enormous. The world's largest oil spill could not have damaged the Great Barrier Reef as much as the crown-of-thorns starfish has damaged it. Millions of coral colonies have been killed, and many more are being destroyed.

How can this problem be solved?

Some scientists suggest that tritons could be raised on a special farm and then turned loose on the reef. They hope that tritons can reduce the numbers of crown-of-thorns starfish in a natural way. Other scientists believe that the crown-of-thorns starfish must be killed one by one. Still others want to wait and see what happens.

Problems with People

The crown-of-thorns starfish is not the only problem on the reef. Just as in other parts of the world, the

A scuba diver displays a piece of staghorn coral. People may be harming the delicate ecosystems of the reef. (Bob Nicol)

ocean life of the Great Barrier Reef is being threatened in many ways. **Sewage** is being pumped into the ocean from coastal cities. Harbors are being dredged and the leftover waste material dumped offshore. **Pesticides** sprayed on farm crops get into streams that flow into the ocean.

Oil companies hold leases covering most of the Great Barrier Reef. Some exploratory wells have been drilled to determine if valuable oil deposits lie beneath the ocean floor.

People have different opinions about how the reef should be used. Some want to use the lime from dead coral for fertilizing crops or in making cement. Others want to blast deeper channels through parts of the reef so that boats can get through. Many people are opposed to these uses of the reef. They argue that parts of the reef are being destroyed, and the delicate balance of ecosystems is being upset.

As more and more tourists come to explore the reef, new buildings are needed to house and feed them. Visitors are collecting more shells and doing more deep-sea fishing, spear fishing, and boating than ever before.

People can and do change the most beautiful natural wonders of the world. Some of these changes are coming to the Great Barrier Reef.

Reef Walking, Scuba Diving, Fishing

A boat load of visitors arrived at Heron Island. Like many of the hundreds of thousands of visitors to the Great Barrier Reef each year, the people in this group wanted to go reef walking.

Walking the Reef

Reef walkers travel across exposed corals at low tide. On the reef the water level changes only about six feet (less than two meters) between high and low tides. Since the top parts of the reef slope down very gradually, large areas are above water at low tide.

Imagine that you have traveled across the world and are ready to begin a reef walk on the Great Barrier Reef. To reef walk, you will need to wear boots or high canvas shoes and to carry a long, sturdy stick. You plunk the stick down ahead of you before you step. It tests the safe places to walk. Otherwise, your foot may break through the upper layers of corals. Then you may find yourself knee-deep in water with nasty

bruises and scratches on your leg.

Starting out on your walk, you explore **tidepools** and look under boulders. A good reef walker will always leave an upturned rock in its same position. Otherwise, the little animals underneath it will be exposed to the sun and die.

As the tide goes farther out, you will see more and more interesting creatures. At least one, the stonefish, can be dangerous to reef walkers. The stonefish lies motionless for long periods on the bottom of coral pools. But, should you happen to step on it while wearing thin-soled shoes, spines on the stonefish's back would inject a strong poison into your feet.

During your walk, you will see tiny fish that are trapped in tidepools until the tide returns. You may see partly opened clams that have bored into the corals by rocking back and forth. They will close as you come near. Wherever you go, you will find shells. If an "empty" shell moves off, a hermit crab probably lives in it.

Along your way you may try to pick up a slimy sea cucumber from one of the tidepools. This foot-long (thirty-one-centimeter-long) creature lies in a circular position and looks like a sausage. It is some-

This young woman enjoys reef walking on the Great Barrier Reef. A good reef walker will leave an upturned rock in its original position.

times called the "vacuum cleaner of the sea" because it eats sand to get its food.

Colorful crayfish, which are delicious to eat, hide beneath the corals on the reef. If you look closely, their antennae give away their hiding places. Unlike the stonefish, the crayfish do not have poisonous spines that will strike at a carelessly placed human foot.

If you walk as far as the outer edge of the reef, the coral platform becomes more solid and easier to walk on. You have now reached the most sturdy part of this big structure. Here, the living corals form a huge wall that holds back the ocean. This part of the reef faces strong winds and violent storms. Weaker parts of this wall have been destroyed by storms and surf. Along the reef edge, while the tide still is ebbing, or going out, small waterfalls drain from the reef into the Pacific Ocean.

You must give yourself plenty of time to return before the tide rises again. If you don't, you may be wading or even swimming with sharks and other large creatures. At night, in order to be sure you can return before the tide changes, you need to carry a waterproof light. You must also arrange for a light to be shining at all times at your starting place.

A reef walker examines a large piece of coral. (Neil Murray)

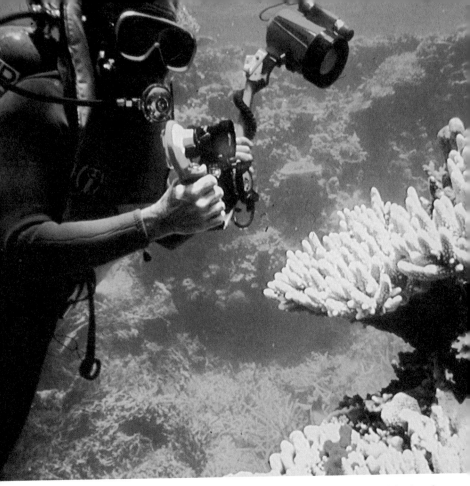

An underwater photographer snaps photographs of several kinds of coral among the waters of the Great Barrier Reef.

Diving and Snorkeling

If you like to **scuba dive**, you have come to the right place. There are more than thirty scuba diving locations to choose from on the Great Barrier Reef.

Diving and snorkeling are popular all over the reef, but Heron Island is a favorite place. On a sunny day when the water is clear and calm, the reef, itself, is very beautiful. For a diver it becomes a background for life within it and near it. Much of the underwater reef is never exposed to the wind and sun. There is much to explore.

As in other places, divers at the reef go down in pairs or groups of three. Before they go underwater, they agree on what each person will do during the dive. For safety, the divers will keep track of each other, stay in a certain area, and surface at a given time. They will also have a boat waiting where they surface. Scuba divers on the reef have to be careful about something else. They make sure their scuba gear does not get hooked on branching corals, which can damage their equipment and cause them to become tangled.

Divers and underwater photographers who dive again and again in the same places get to know some of the individual reef animals. Sometimes they even give them names such as "Morey" the moray eel or "Angie" the angelfish. The divers often see these creatures each time they dive in the same spot. Because living space is hard to find on the Great Barrier Reef, many of the smaller animals live out their lives in a very small area.

Boats and Black Marlin

The reef can be a challenge to those who attempt to pass through it in boats. Some reef areas are so difficult to navigate that only a few skilled skippers take boats through them. These people know that when tides drop, sometimes corals and boat bottoms meet.

Because of the problems of navigation, only fishing and pearling boats reach most parts of the Great Barrier Reef. Still, many other places remain for Australians and visitors to enjoy. Through glass-bottom boats and boats with underwater glass cabins, visitors view the wonders of undersea life in the reef. Green Island also has an underwater observatory that many visitors enjoy.

Many anglers dream of deep-sea fishing at the Great Barrier Reef. When they actually come here to fish, they are not disappointed. Charter services take anglers out from the mainland and from tourist resorts. They stay for a day or longer in places where they can catch coral trout, cod, snappers, wrasses, and other game fish.

Many anglers like to fish on the quiet side of the reef. Others prefer the more rugged side where the

This view of corals on the Great Barrier Reef was taken through the bottom of a glass-bottom boat. (Neil Murray)

Great Barrier Reef meets the ocean. Some anglers use **echo sounders** to help locate fish by searching for corals in deeper waters off the reef. Still others like to drift in the channels among the reefs.

From September through November each year, black marlin migrate through the reefs. This is a special time for big-game anglers. Each year during this season they catch many marlins. Rather than keep these fish, though, the anglers release most of them into the waters of the reef.

A Marine Park for the Future

In the 1970s the people of Australia decided that the Great Barrier Reef needed to be protected. They were especially concerned about threats to reef creatures. As a result, the Australian government passed the Great Barrier Reef Marine Park Act of 1975. This law established new rules to protect the reef and its plants and animals.

In 1979 Australia created the Great Barrier Reef Marine Park at the southern end of the reef. This small part of the reef is now protected from underwater mining, drilling, and other development. The park has a marine research center and a bird **sanctuary** that

A coral island rises from the sea in the Great Barrier Reef.

provides a refuge for more than 17,000 birds.

People all over the world come to the marine park to enjoy the natural wonders of the Great Barrier Reef. Foreign visitors and Australians want to preserve the reef's beauty for future generations. For them and many others, it is truly a treasure in the sea.

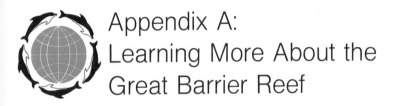

Appendix A:
Learning More About the
Great Barrier Reef

The following activities will help you to learn more about the Great Barrier Reef. Choose one or more to begin working on today.

1. Read a biography of Captain James Cook. Why did his experience on North Sea coasters help him get the *Endeavour* safely out of the reefs? On a map, trace the route Captain Cook sailed to reach the Great Barrier Reef.

2. Draw and color a picture to show how fish are camouflaged. Include brightly colored fish living among coral reefs and darkly colored fish living in lagoons. Show that the fish are almost invisible in their surroundings.

3. Visit a saltwater aquarium or a tropical fish store. What colors are the fish and other creatures? Notice whether certain fish prefer to swim at certain levels. If these fish were at the Great Barrier Reef, which do you think would live near the water's surface? Which would live deeper? Which would live among the corals? Which would live in the lagoons?

4. Start a notebook showing creatures of the Great Barrier Reef. Include those that live in the water, on land, and in the air. Write something interesting about each one.

Appendix B:
Scientific Names
for Sea Animals

Sea creatures, like all living things, have two kinds of names. The first is their *common name*, a name in the everyday language of an area where they are found. An animal often has a number of different common names in different languages. Also, several different animals may be known by the same common name.

The second kind of name is their *scientific name*. This is a Latin name assigned by scientists to identify an animal all over the world for other scientists. The scientific name is usually made up of two words. The first identifies a genus, or group, of similar animals (or plants), and the second identifies the species, or kind, of animal in the group. Sometimes, as scientists learn more about an animal, they may decide it belongs to a different group. The scientific name is then changed so that all scientists can recognize it and know exactly what animal it refers to.

If you want to learn more about the creatures in this book, the list of scientific names below will be useful to you. A typical species has been identified for each type of animal mentioned in the book. There may be many other species in the same group.

Chapter	Common Name	Scientific Name
1.	Reef Starlet Coral	*Siderastrea siderea*
2.	Stingray	*Dasyatis sayi*
	Dugong	*Dugong dugon*
3.	Blue-banded Angelfish	*Pygoplites diacanthus*
	Common Octopus	*Octopus vulgaris*
	Wobbegong (Carpet Shark)	*Orectolobus maculatus*
	Stonefish	*Synanceja horrida*
	Remora	*Echeneis naucrates*
	Manta Ray	*Manta birostris*
	Trumpetfish	*Aulostomus chinensis*
	Sand Shrimp	*Crangon vulgaris*
	Common Prawn	*Palaemonetes vulgaris*
	Lionfish	*Pterois volitans*
	Nudibranch	*Dentronotus frondosus*
	Purple Urchin	*Arbacia punctulata*

Chapter	Common Name	Scientific Name
	Gall Crab	*Haplocarcinus marsupialis*
	Common Starfish	*Asterias forbesi*
	Brittle Star	*Ophioscolex glacialis*
	Cleaner Wrasse	*Thalassoma bifasciatum*
	Blenny	*Aspidonotus taeniatus*
	Sea Anemone	*Metridium dianthus*
	Clownfish	*Amphiprion percula*
	Sea Slug	*Cyerce nigra*
	Snapping Shrimp	*Synalpheus brooksi*
4.	Wedge-tailed Shearwater	*Puffinus tenuirostris*
	Moray Eel	*Muraena helena*
	Great White Heron	*Ardea occidentalis*
	Ghost Crab	*Ocypode albicans*
	Dog Whelk	*Nassa trivittata*
	Feather Star	*Heliometra glacialis*

Chapter	Common Name	Scientific Name
	Common Eastern Chiton	*Chaetopleura apiculata*
	Scorpion Fish	*Scorpaena scrofa*
	Damselfish	*Abudefduf saxatilis*
	Mackerel	*Scomber scombrus*
	Herring	*Clupea harengus*
	Mullet	*Mugil cephalus*
	Barracuda	*Sphyraena barracuda*
	Snapper	*Lutjanus blackfordi*
5.	Small Hermit Crab	*Pagurus longicarpus*
	Cowrie	*Cyprae spodicea*
	Parrotfish	*Scarus guacamaia*
	Squirrelfish	*Holocentrus ascensionis*
	Cardinal	*Apogon hyalosoma*
	Butterfly Fish	*Teuthis hepatus*
	Brown Sea Cucumber	*Thyone briareus*

Chapter	Common Name	Scientific Name
6.	Green Sea Turtle	*Chelonia mydas*
	Common Squid	*Loligo pealei*
	Noddy Tern (white-capped)	*Anous albus*
	Frigate Bird	*Fregata magnificens*
7.	Crown-of-thorns Starfish	*Acanthaster planci*
	Triton	*Fusitriton oregonensis*
	Queensland Grouper	*Promicrops lanceolatus*
8.	Crayfish	*Cambarus bartoni*
	Cod	*Gadus callarias*
	Blue Marlin	*Makaira nigricans*

 Glossary

algae (AL-jee)—any of a group of mainly aquatic plants, such as seaweed, pond scum, and stonewort, often masked by a brown or red pigment

antennae (an-TEHN-ee)—used here to describe sense organs on the head of small crustaceans

ballast—heavy material carried in a ship to make it more stable in the water

billion—a thousand million; written as 1,000,000,000

breakwater—a heavy wall, or barrier, that provides protection from large waves

calcium (KAL-see-uhm)—a silver-white metallic element; coral polyps take calcium from seawater and change it into a rocky lime skeleton

camouflage (KAM-uh-flahzh)—used here to describe a creature's attempt to disguise itself by looking like its surroundings

cays (KAYS)—low-lying islands of coral or sand

continental shelf—the shallow underwater plain, varying in width, that extends out into the ocean from each of the world's continents

corals—sea animals with hard, rocklike skeletons on the outside of their bodies; huge numbers of coral polyps massed together form coral reefs by building on the hardened skeletons of past generations

crevices (KREV-ih-sez)—narrow openings resulting from splits or cracks

crustaceans (kruhs-TAY-shuhns)—lobsters, shrimps, crabs and other mostly marine animals of a large class, Crustacea

cycle—a course or series of events that occur regularly and usually lead back to the same starting point

cyclones—storms that rotate around a center of low pressure and often bring high winds and driving rain

digestive system—the parts of an animal in which food is absorbed by dissolving it

dissolve—to break down a substance into the parts of which it is made

echo sounder—a device used in locating fish that pinpoints the location of an underwater object by means of sound waves reflected back to it from the object

ecology (ee-KAHL-uh-jee)—the relationship of animals, plants, and their environment; a change in any one of these parts affects the others

ecosystems (EHK-oh-sis-tuhms)—natural communities of plants, animals, and nonliving things and the ways in which they influence each other. Ecosystems can be very large, like the planet Earth, or small, like a rotting log

endangered species (SPEE-sheez)—a species, or distinct kind of plant or animal, that is in danger of becoming extinct

environment—used here to mean all living and nonliving things, conditions, and influences—temperature, movement of the water, and neighboring plants and animals, for example—within a certain area in the sea or on land

erode—to wear away by the action of water, wind, or ice; waves erode weaker parts of the Great Barrier Reef

fertilize (FUR-tuh-lize)—to combine a sperm and egg to begin the process that gives life to a new creature; also, to apply fertilizer to plants to help them grow

gastric sac (GAS-trik SAK)—stomach; the crown-of-thorns starfish uses its gastric sac to cover, dissolve, and absorb corals on the Great Barrier Reef

gills—breathing organs that filter oxygen from seawater for sea animals

Ice Age—a cold period in earth history when glacial ice covered large areas of the world

lagoons (luh-GOONS)—shallow channels, sounds, or ponds that are near or connected with large bodies of water

larva (plural—larvae [LAHR-vee])—the early form of an animal that at birth or hatching is unlike its parent and must change before it becomes an adult

lime—used here to describe a rocky substance produced by coral polyps from the calcium in seawater

mantle—used here to describe the living tissue of the cowrie that can extend around the shell's sides to clean, rub, and polish the shell

microscopic (my-kro-SCOP-ik)—extremely small in size; an object that can be seen only with a microscope

migrate—to go, in certain seasons, from one region or climate to another for feeding or breeding. Many birds migrate each year over long distances

mollusks (MAHL-uhsks)—snails, clams, and other animals with soft bodies, no backbones, and usually protected by hard, outer shells

nettle-cells—cells that contain a stinging fluid

nutrients (NYU-tree-ents)—substances that promote the growth of living things. Plankton are rich in nutrients

oakum—loose hemp or jute fiber that was used to caulk, or fill in, seams in wooden ships centuries ago when Captain Cook sailed the oceans

oxygen-rich water—used here to mean water that contains more oxygen than normal seawater

paralyze (PAHR-uh-lize)—to make powerless or unable to move normally

parasites (PAHR-uh-sites)—often harmful creatures that live in or on other creatures

pesticides (PEHS-tuh-sides)—chemical substances used to destroy pests

phytoplankton (fyt-oh-PLANK-tuhn)—tiny plants that drift in the ocean and become the food of many animals

pitch—a tarlike substance used by Captain Cook's crew to help repair their damaged ship

plankton—tiny plants and animals that float or drift in the sea; many are microscopic

plumb—used here to mean dropping weighted line in the water to measure the distance to the bottom

predators (PREHD-uh-tuhrs)—creatures that seek and kill other animals for food

prey (PRAY)—animals taken by a predator as food

radula (RAJ-uh-lah)—the ribbonlike tongue with tiny, scraping teeth found in some mollusks such as marine snails

reef flats—the somewhat flat top part of a coral reef that is exposed when the tide goes out

sanctuary (SANK-chuh-wuhr-ee)—used here to describe a place where wildlife is protected from human activities

secrete (sih-KREET)—to form and give off a substance

sediment (SED-uh-muhnt)—used here to describe materials that settle to the ocean bottom

sewage—liquid or solid waste matter carried off by sewers and usually processed at sewage treatment plants

shoal—a large group; some fish swim in shoals

sounding—measuring the depth of water by means of a weighted line

species (SPEE-sheez)—distinct kinds of individual plants or animals that have common characteristics and share a common name

symbiosis (sihm-by-OH-sihs)—the living together of two kinds of animals or plants for their mutual benefit

tentacles (TEHN-tuh-kuhls)—armlike extensions on a sea animal's body; used for moving, feeling, or grasping

territorial (tuhr-uh-TOR-ee-uhl)—used here to describe an animal that defends the area around its home

tidepool—a pool of seawater in which sea creatures are captive until the tide comes in and allows them to leave

zooplankton (zoh-uh-PLANK-tuhn)—tiny animals that feed on phytoplankton floating in the sea

Selected Bibliography

Books

Clare, Patricia. *The Struggle for the Great Barrier Reef.* New York: Walker, 1971.

Clarke, Arthur C. *The Coast of Coral.* New York: Harper, 1955.

Endean, Robert. *Australia's Great Barrier Reef.* St. Lucia, Queensland, Australia: University of Queensland Press, 1982.

McGregor, Craig, and the editors of Time-Life Books. *The Great Barrier Reef: The World's Wild Places.* New York: Time-Life Books, 1974.

Zim, Herbert S., and Krantz, Lucretia. *Sea Stars and Their Kin.* New York: Morrow Junior Books, 1976.

Articles

Abbey, Edward. "Man and the Great Reef." *Audubon*, January 1972.

Connell, Des. "Australia's Great Barrier Reef National Park." *Sea Frontiers*, July/August 1980.

MacLeish, Kenneth. "Australia's Great Barrier Reef" and "Exploring Australia's Coral Jungle." *National Geographic* , June 1973.

Sisson, Robert F. "Life Cycle of a Coral." *National Geographic*, June 1973.

Sterba, James P. "To the Great Barrier Reef and Beyond." *New York Times Magazine,* July 25, 1982.

Summerhays, Soames. "A Marine Park is Born." *National Geographic,* May 1981.

Taylor, Ron and Valerie. "Paradise Beneath the Sea." *National Geographic,* May 1981.

 Index

About the Author

Alice Gilbreath is the author of eighteen previous books for young people during a twenty-year writing career. Her wide-ranging interests have led her to write about numerous subjects, from beginning crafts to the defensive techniques of animals.

"In writing this book," says the author, "I wanted to share with young people the uniqueness and beauty of the reef and its inhabitants. How marvelous it is that creatures half an inch long have built a barrier that holds back the mighty Pacific Ocean! And what an inspiration these tiny creatures are for our own lives. When we understand them, we can better understand our own potential."

Ms. Gilbreath attended Trinity University in San Antonio, the University of Tulsa, and the College of Idaho. She lives in Bartlesville, Oklahoma.